Crea[illegible] Writing

Written by Jim Symonds
Illustrated by Mandy Doyle

HENDERSON
PUBLISHING LTD

DEAR NOEL...

Many famous stories begin in unusual ways. The well-loved tales of Beatrix Potter began with a letter to a sick child. Beatrix knew a little boy called Noel and she decided to cheer him up by writing him a letter.

In the letter, she wrote a story about the adventures of a naughty little rabbit called Peter who got up to all sorts of mischief. There were pretty illustrations in the margins and on the envelope.

Noel got better and the letter was put in a drawer under his jumpers. It was only years later that a vicar saw the letter and thought the story of Peter Rabbit was too good to be hidden in a drawer and it was published. The rest is history!

ABSENT MINDED

A famous writer called T. E. Lawrence (also known as Lawrence of Arabia) had just finished a very long book called "Seven Pillars of Wisdom". He took it on the train to his publishers but left it on his seat when he got off at the station. The book was never found and as it was in the days before word processors, he had to write it all over again!

READY, STEADY..GO!

Some writers have taken up to twenty years to complete a story or a poem and the finished result isn't always that brilliant! But **YOU** don't need long to write a masterpiece. You can write a poem in a matter of seconds!

What you need:

- a friend with a watch (it must have a second hand)
- a pen that works (or a SHARP pencil)
- some paper

What you do:
Before you start your timed poem, think about a title. It needs to be something that really grabs you, not something boring like "Autumn."
Try one of these for starters;

"My neighbours"

"Blizzard"

"At midnight"

"School dinners"

Write down the title before you start. Then choose the number of seconds that you're going to write for and tell your friend. Between 100 and 150 seconds is good for the first attempt.

School dinners

School dinners are absolutely gross
They have mushed up beans
and fiddly little peas
The only thing I like about school dinners
is walking out of the hall
when you've had them!

Oliver, aged 1(
(121 seconds

You will find that because you have so little time you will write almost immediately and your finished poem will sound fresh. Don't worry about rhyme unless you want to. When you get the hang of 'timed' poetry, choose some titles of your own but make sure they are unusual and stimulating!

Copy out and decorate your poems at leisure. Show them to your friends and see if they can guess how long it took you to write them!

Mini stories

Some stories are millions of words long but are all those words really needed? See if you can write a complete story in less than 50 words! Choose something exciting to write about. It could be a ghost story or even a love story!

Have a beginning, middle and end. Pick your words carefully and don't repeat yourself - you can't afford to! You might like to copy your story into a little book with not too many words on each page and lots of illustrations.

UNUSUAL IDEAS

Make up your own alphabet
Ever get bored of using the same old 26 letters whenever you write anything? Well, why not use your own? There are hundreds of different alphabets throughout the world so one more won't make much difference!

You could use:
patterns, shapes, squiggles, colours, pictures to represent each of the 26 letters of our own alphabet. Then you can use your 'personal' alphabet to write messages, letters, stories and poems. See if your friends can work out what you have written. Tell them the secret of some of your alphabet but not all of it and see if they can work out the rest!

HIDDEN MESSAGES

Many stories that you read are about the search for something. It might be a person, a place or even treasure. Often there are messages along the way which help the characters in the story find what they are looking for. It can be fun to hide something and then leave a series of messages to help friends search for what YOU have hidden.

1. Go into the garden, find the magic tree and walk around it.

You could start by choosing something like an old tin box filled with pennies and hide it in a garden behind a tree. The first message might be in a bedroom and could lead your friends to another one hidden in the kitchen;

"Go down the stairs and out into the garden. Look for the tallest tree and walk slowly around it."

You could try writing each message backwards or with your 'personal' alphabet to make it really tricky to understand where the treasure is hidden!

Thin Poems
If you want to write poems about 'things that go bump in the night', then it's a good idea to write them in a thin shape to add to the tension and drama of being scared!

Make a list of frightening words before you start, like; lonely, suddenly, screaming, creepy, howling. If possible, copy your 'creepy poem' onto black paper with gold or silver pens and decorate it with cobwebs and stars!

GHOST STORIES

If you want to write a good ghost story, it's important that there is plenty of tension, as if something is always about to happen! Try to use lots of short sentences and include plenty of detail; "The grandfather clock chimed midnight. But I couldn't sleep. Somewhere I could hear footsteps. The wind blew fiercely outside. I was not alone in the room but I could see no-one."

When you finish, you could read your story onto a tape and make some sound effects with everyday household objects like combs, a creaky door or a noisy pet! Read your story slowly and clearly with a spooky voice!

WEIRD and WONDERFUL

Here are some rather peculiar ideas for creative writing that you might like to try out. These activities might even help you to think of some more ideas of your own!

What you need:
- a bag of mints
- white paper,felt pens or pencils.
- scissors and a saucer (or something round.)

Inventing Words
It's always good fun to think of a word that isn't already in the dictionary. Don't forget, new words are being invented all the time, so why not join in the fun? Here's a simple idea to get you started.

What you do:
Suck a mint slowly and write down all the words, sounds and feelings that come into your mind as you do. The strong taste should make you think of unusual, new words. For instance; fizzburning, coldwaterwanting, mouthtingling...the list is endless! Don't worry about spelling. These are your words so you can spell them just how you want to! When you have finished, cut out a circle of white paper and copy out your invented words using bright colours. You might also like to be inspired by raw onion or food of your own choice!

NEWSPAPER FUN

You can have great fun making stories, poems and curious sentences out of words and phrases from old newspapers or magazines. It does take time but the different sorts of typeface can make the final result look very effective!

What you need:

- old newspapers or magazines
- scissors
- glue
- a large sheet of plain paper.

What you do:
Search through the papers and look for words and phrases that you find interesting. When you have collected all you want, begin to arrange your words on a large piece of plain paper. Don't stick anything down until you're happy with what you've created.

softer WRITE
sensational
a breath of fresh air is
And now for something completely different...
EXCITING
with
SECRET GARDEN
beautifully crazy! good
BEST
AND
RELAXING
with
Three cheers

You might need to search back through the papers for joining words like 'and' or 'but'- don't forget you can make these words by just cutting up longer ones!

You might like to illustrate your story or poem with pictures from colour magazines.

TURNING JAPANESE

As you know, the Japanese are very fond of small things. Haikus are VERY small poems that came across from Japan at the turn of the century. You can have great fun writing them!

A Haiku is a poem of three lines. There are seventeen syllables (beats) altogether; five in the first line, seven in the second and five in the third. Your title can be as long as you like.

Haikus are like little "snapshots" of life. If you haven't got a camera, write a Haiku! Here are some useful subjects to 'snap' with words; a rainbow, a sunset, a storm, a yawning cat, crunching through the fresh fallen snow...

Haikus are good poems because they squeeze all your thoughts into a tiny little space. There is no chance for the reader to get bored! You can even repeat the first line at the end to give it a nice pattern and to make the words sound musical;

Copy your Haikus onto best quality paper. If you have a calligraphy pen, then here's the right time to use it. Bring out the beauty and simplicity of your poem with lovely handwriting and delicate pictures. The Japanese would definitely approve!

Helpful hint

If you aren't too sure how many 'beats' there are in a certain word, then say it aloud and tap with your finger at the same time; e.g..

Tor-toise = 2 syllables.
Beau-ti-ful = 3 syllables.
Fish = 1 syllable.

INTO THE UNKNOWN

Some writers can take simply ages working out the plot and title of their stories, but here's an idea that will solve this problem almost immediately! This activity works best in small groups but it can work well in pairs and even on your own!

What you need:

- lots of small pieces of paper (each about the size of half a postcard),
- writing paper
- pens or pencils
- three open containers (you could use waste baskets or cardboard boxes).

What you do:
Label the three containers:
1. 'Titles', 2. 'People', 3. 'Places'.

Now you need to fill each container with as many small pieces of paper as possible. On each piece of paper there will be an idea for a title, person or place in a story. When you have written an idea, fold it carefully (so it can't be read) and pop it into the correct container. The stranger the idea, the better the story will be!

Here are some examples for you;

1. Titles
"The fish that couldn't swim."
"A wet day in March."
"The upside-down shop."

2. People
"Bugs bunny."
"A lady in a tea shop called Doris."
"The smallest monster in Birmingham."

3. Places
"A jumble sale."
"The King's dining room."
"Behind a settee in Scotland."

The more ideas you have, the better it will be for your stories! What do you do now? Shake up the contents of each container and pick out a piece of folded paper from each one so that you have a title, a character and a setting for your story. You are going to have to use all your creative skills to find a way to join these different ideas into one plot! The story might begin like this;

"A Wet Day in March"

Once there was a LADY IN A TEA SHOP CALLED DORIS who spent all her spare time eating crumpets with honey. One day, she was walking to A JUMBLE SALE when rain began to fall heavily.
"I mustn't get my hair wet," she said and.......

After a few goes, you might want to pick out two or even three people or places from your containers to make your story even more of a challenge to write!

Now and again, change the ideas in the containers to keep your stories fresh. Copy out your favourite ones and illustrate them with zany pictures.

CREATIVE DREAMING

In our dreams we can imagine anything. Many great ideas for stories have begun with a dream, so why not use them for some creative writing?

Dream book
It could be a good idea to have a 'Dream Book' beside your bed so that if you wake up from an amazing dream you can quickly jot it down on paper. You must remember that dreams are about the easiest things to forget, so if you write them down, you can use them later in your stories or poems if you want.

You can draw scenes from your dreams, too!

Day-dreaming
Many of you will spend part of your DAY dreaming, too. When your teacher thinks you are hard at work on some dead boring maths, you may be miles away having a much more interesting time in the world of your day dreams!

"My teacher thinks I'm doing my long division-but I'm not! I'm sailing in a red balloon over a forest of lions!"

Julie(aged 9)

You could use this word pattern, "My teacher thinks..." and make up some verses of your own! Or use another word pattern, like;

"I MIGHT BE lining up for dinners, BUT REALLY I'm in my tree house with my dog and a toffee apple."

You might like to illustrate these 'day dream' poems with pictures of what you are doing and pictures of what you're DREAMING of doing!

THAT'S SURREAL, MAN!

Have you ever seen a cow play the piano, or a settee with real legs running down a hill? Well, if you're a surrealist you might have done! They're artists who let the world of their dreams take over their paintings. They show 'impossible' things as if they are very possible! Try cutting out pictures from magazines and have a go at making a surreal collage; you could use animals, furniture, famous people, kitchen objects, etc.

When you finish, write a poem or story to go with your picture.

"IMAGINE A WORLD with fish playing cards and hens riding bicycles...

You could use the word pattern "IMAGINE A WORLD..." or "I DREAMT I SAW..." for each verse. If you decide to write a story to go with your surreal picture, you could end it with "...and then I woke up!"

DEAR DIARY

Nearly all famous writers have kept a diary at some time in their lives, and some diaries are very famous indeed, even if their authors aren't famous writers! Some of you will have heard of Anne Frank, who as a young girl wrote a diary in Holland during the second world war before she was killed.

Diaries can be wonderful because they keep you writing and show you many things about yourself and others as you grow older. If you haven't started one yet, then why not start one today?

What sort?

1. Yearly diary: This gives you one page for each day of the year but sometimes (on quiet days) you don't need a whole page and other times (when a lot happens) you need more than a page!

2. Five year diary: On each page there is the same day for five successive years. This can make it very interesting to see immediately what you were doing 'this time last year', but usually there is hardly any space for writing!

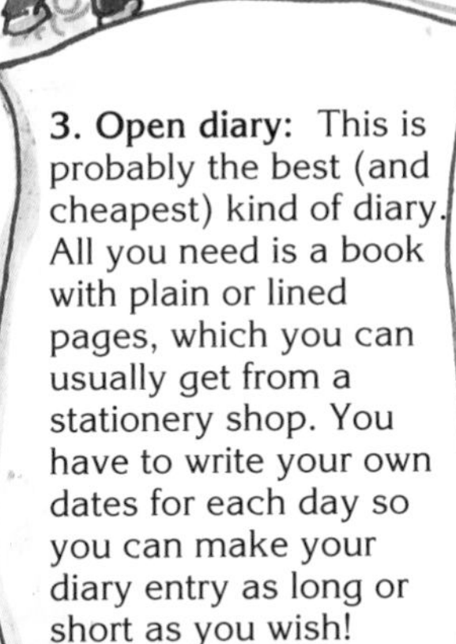

3. Open diary: This is probably the best (and cheapest) kind of diary. All you need is a book with plain or lined pages, which you can usually get from a stationery shop. You have to write your own dates for each day so you can make your diary entry as long or short as you wish!

"Dear diary, today was boring."
One of the most important skills of a writer is to make things that seem boring really interesting. Even though some days are more exciting than others, there is never a completely boring day. Even if you are poorly in bed, you can listen to what's happening outside the window or imagine what's happening at school! Write it all down!

Soft, strong and

Some stories have been written on the back of an envelope, some written in the sand on a sunny beach. Why not write yours on ... loo roll?

A 'long story' can take on a new meaning! You could write a story that stretches from your bedroom to the kitchen and beyond. Make sure you only write one long line so that the story goes as far as possible!

Make sure you use a thin felt tip pen for your story; a biro will tear the paper and a pencil won't show up.

Of course, you could use any roll of paper that you might have lying about...

Possible titles:

The long journey to the misty mountain.

The cat that walked all the way to the moon.

etc.

STORY ON A TAPE

If you've written a genuinely LENGTHY story, then you might like to record it onto a tape. You might even get some of your friends to speak the parts of some of the characters, or you could disguise your own voice and read all the parts yourself! Turn the tape player off every so often to have a rest so that your story always sounds fresh. You could even have a break for some adverts - either make them up or record them off the telly!

If you're somebody who has great ideas for a story but finds it difficult to write things down, then a story tape is the thing for you!

When you have recorded your story (or stories), you could cut some white card to fit into the tape box and decorate it with bright felt tip pens to make your story tape look really professional!

Why not then make some 'back up' tapes and send them to your friends?

OUT AND ABOUT

Long journeys

When was the last time you spent hours sitting in the back of a car with nothing to do other than tickle the person sitting next to you?

Wherever you're travelling, there are always things of interest to be seen outside the window and the skill of a writer is to be able to notice these things, whatever they are!

Make a habit of carrying a little book and pencil to note things down that can be turned into a piece of writing later.

101 things to see out of a car window.

A lady yawning at a bus stop
Three children laughing in a park
The door of a hairdresser's being slammed

by Kevin (aged 9)

You could use the same idea for a bus or train ride. Apart from being creative, it will also make the journey go quicker!

Then and now

It can be interesting to see how times have changed over the years. If you have an elderly relative or friend of the family who remembers what life was like a long time ago, you could go and visit them with a tape recorder and ask about their memories of childhood and record what they have to say!

Prepare some questions before you set off, such as; What games did you play? What was school like? What did you do in the holidays? etc.

When you bring the tape home, have a listen; some parts will be more interesting than others so decide which 'bits' you want to copy out! Use the pause button on the tape player so you don't have to copy too much out at one time!

Now you can write about the games YOU play, what you do at school and in the holidays to show how times have changed over the years. You might like to make a little book called 'Then and Now'. Maybe you'll find that some things have hardly changed at all!

At the Zoo

Do you like writing stories and poems about animals? Next time you go to the zoo, take a little notebook and when you find your favourite animals, see how carefully you can describe them!

Try to find 10 ways to describe a lion's yawn or 7 ways to describe the smell of a skunk! It could be fun and will help to improve powers of description in your animal writing!

THE SEASONS

Each season brings with it ideas for creative writing. Here are some ideas to get you started.

Winter
The Eskimos are so used to snow that they have over 40 different words to describe it! We only have 'snow' and 'sludge' but there are many other words that come to mind when we think of snow; crunch, Christmas, boots, cold, white...

When it snows, make a list of all the words that come to mind...you might want to include words that you've made up! For instance, a word to describe the sound of walking through freshly-fallen snow. You'll probably end up with more words than the Eskimos!

Arrange the words to make up a poem. If you use white chalk on black paper you can have the words falling from the sky like real snowflakes!

Spring
Writers usually go on about how beautiful the Spring is, so it would be quite fun to find things to really dislike about it!

You could write a poem called "Yuck! It's Spring!" or, "17 Good reasons to dislike Spring." Your own titles will probably be best.

You could also write a poem in praise of Spring to see if it's easier to be nice about Spring than nasty about it!

Summer
If you are at the seaside, you could write a little poem in the sand and then photograph it before the sea washes the words away!

You might like to try writing a Haiku (see page 11) about a day at the seaside;

The sound of the sea
is drowned by the
voices of children on
the beach.

You could decorate your sand poem with shells and seaweed. Make sure your shadow doesn't get in the photograph!

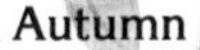

Autumn
Collect some 'Autumny things' like leaves, conkers and blackberries. Imagine you are one of these things and write a story describing what it's like for you when Autumn comes. Don't actually say what you are and see if friends can guess when they read your story!

"One windy day I fell gently onto the forest floor. There I lay with my friends. It was damp but we were warm. Then one day I was picked up, carried home and placed into a book..."

Later, you could copy out your story onto a piece of paper that you've cut into the shape of the 'Autumny thing' that you've described!

FANCY THAT!

The Martians have landed!
In 1938 the film director Orson Wells decided to make a radio play of the H.G.Wells science fiction classic "War of the Worlds" which tells the story of a Martian invasion during a war between Earth and Mars.

The play was broadcast throughout America and it was so lifelike that many people thought there really was a Martian invasion. They panicked and ran out into the streets, crying "The Martians have landed!"

It was only some hours later that they realised it was only a story!

Teacher and pupil
Before he became a famous writer, H.G.Wells was a science teacher. One of his pupils was a little boy who also had dreams of writing a book one day. His name was A. A. Milne who was later to write "Winnie-the-Pooh." Piglet would certainly have been frightened if he knew his creator had been taught by a man who wrote about creatures from outer space!!

Shortest letter ever!

When Victor Hugo, a famous French writer who lived about the same time as Charles Dickens, had finished writing his incredibly long book "Les Miserables," he was very tired so he decided to go to Italy for a holiday! After a while, he became curious about how well his new book was selling, so he wrote to his publishers in Paris,"?". A short time later came the reply from Paris which was simply,"!"

Story competition

Mary Shelley was only eighteen years old when she went on holiday to the mountains with a group of famous writers. During that time, it snowed so heavily that it was impossible to leave the cottage where they were all staying.

Everybody decided to tell a ghost story to pass the time. Mary's was so brilliant that when she returned to England she copied it out and sent it to the publishers who accepted it!

The name of the ghost story was "Frankenstein".

FRESH IDEAS FOR PLAYS

Writing plays

Probably the most important thing to remember when you write a play is to have a fresh line for every 'new' person who speaks; e.g.

PETER: Can you hear a noise coming from that old chest?

MICHAEL: What sort of noise?

PETER: A sort of 'Oooh!'

MICHAEL: Don't be silly. Trunks can't make a noise - unless they're elephant trunks!

The reason for this is, it makes it easier for the characters in a play to say their own lines and not the lines of someone else! But writing plays in this way will also help you when you want to have characters speaking in stories - except there you have to remember to use speech marks!

Another useful idea when writing plays is to have stage directions written in a different colour (or in a different style of handwriting). If they stand out clearly they will be remembered and not read out by mistake!

THE CHEST SLOWLY OPENS. PETER AND MICHAEL DO NOT NOTICE!

You might also want to have a NARRATOR in your play. A narrator sets the scene and describes some of the events in the play but doesn't normally talk to the other characters!

Before you start, have a look at some other plays to give you some more ideas about layout (what a play actually looks like when it's written down). But the most important thing is having good ideas. Shakespeare often let other people write down his plays for him!

Radio plays
You could record your play onto a tape and 'do' all the characters in different voices! Why not have intervals and make up some silly adverts?

T.V. Plays
A good way to get started is to choose a well-known story such as "Snow White" or "The Three Little Pigs", and write a crazy version of it as a play! Snow White could be a really nasty piece of work or the pigs could be hippies!

You could make a pretend T.V. out of a big cardboard box and use bears and dolls as characters so that you can play all the parts yourself!

Weird plays
Why don't you write an incredibly short play which lasts less than a minute? Or a play where the characters are lamp posts or cushions? Or a play where the characters make noises but say no words? All these sorts of plays have been written by peculiar playwrights so why not join in?

Create your own world
The Bronte sisters, who are famous for their books 'Jane Eyre' and 'Wuthering Heights', began writing as children by describing their fantasy worlds, called 'Gondal' and 'Angria'.

They lived on the wild Yorkshire moors and spent many long days in their attic, living in the worlds they had created. Their father had given them 12 toy soldiers and they added houses, hills and roads.

Hundreds of stories came from the adventures of the people of 'Gondal' and 'Angria'. Their father probably had to call loudly to get them to come downstairs for their supper!
You might like to try and create your own fantasy world. You could use some of your toys and make whole streets out of boxes and other odds and ends. You might even want to add a model railway!

Give your world a special name. It won't have to follow the rules of our own world so it's up to you to decide what rules, if any, to have!

Maybe your fantasy world only exists when nobody else is there. You can start by writing descriptions of all the major characters and the most important places. Put all your writing in a special book and keep it hidden in one of the buildings!

FANTASTIC FAIRY TALES

Fairy stories are filled with fantasy; witches, castles, magic spells..the list is endless. But a fairy story only has one ending. How boring! Why not have six?

What to do:
Before you start, have a good look at some fairy stories (especially those of Hans Anderson) to fill your mind with fantastic ideas. Write the beginning and middle of your story but not the end;

"The Prince walked towards the castle in the moonlight. He opened the door and..."

Now the reader of your fairy story is going to have to roll a dice to see what happens next! Write six different endings to your story. You can make them all incredibly different because ANYTHING is possible in a fairy story!

So if someone rolls a 4, the story might continue like this;

"He opened the door and...a huge troll was standing there with eyes the size of saucepans. The Prince ran between his legs..."

You might want to make your own dice with special symbols on each face (like a moon or a star) to make your fairy story even more fantastic!

If you're feeling really clever, you could have a choice of six beginnings or even six middles but you must make sure that the story fits together at the end. If six is too many then use a coin and have two choices!

Dictionary Game
Look in some big dictionaries for weird and peculiar words that your friends won't know. Write down the word and its meaning but don't show it to anybody!

Here's an example;
GORAL, which is an Indian antelope.

What you do;
Invent some other possible meanings of the word you've chosen so that the real meaning is hidden amongst your made-up meanings. So, GORAL could also mean;

a fish with a poisonous sting,

a mountain with a flat top,

a cheese soup from Denmark,

Try and make sure that your 'made-up meanings' sound as if they might be true. Then read out all the meanings to friends and see if they can guess the real one!

You might turn this into a game so that friends get a point if they guess correctly and you get a point if they don't! It can be great fun and you'll also be learning new words!

Write the meanings onto bits of paper and add little illustrations if you want; make sure you don't giggle when you read out one of the 'made up meanings' because that'll give the game away!

S.W.A.L.K!
You've probably seen this written on the back of an envelope and you no doubt know it stands for "Sealed with a loving kiss!"

There are secret messages hidden inside all sorts of words and sometimes the message helps to remember the spelling of the word; e.g.,

G.L.A.S.G.O.W.=
Granny Likes A Small Glass Of Wine!

These hidden messages are called mnemonics. Try and make up some of your own, however silly or strange they might be!

L.O.N.D.O.N.=
Let Our Noses Dance On Noodles!

You can make up mnemonics for place names or for people's names. Why not illustrate them with peculiar pictures to help you remember them?

Palindromes
A palindrome is a word or phrase that reads the same backwards and forwards, such as Mum or Dad. But there are some very long palindromes, such as "Ten animals I slam in a net!"

Start a collection of palindromes and amaze your friends with them, especially if you have a friend called Hannah!

ESPECIALLY FOR YOU

You might have seen those books where the name and address of somebody has been printed into the story to make it look as if the story has been written especially for them. They are normally given to you as Christmas or birthday presents. But you don't need to send lots of money to a publishing company when you can write a special story for a friend yourself and it can be a much better story!

What you do: Choose who you want to write a story for; it might be your classmate, your little sister or your penfriend who lives by the seaside. Make a list of questions to ask which will help you plan your story. These might include;

"Do you have any favourite names for the characters in your story?"

"Where would you like your story to be set; the countryside, the seaside, a city, outer space?"

"What sort of story do you like best; ghost story, adventure story, love story, murder story?"

"Do you want your story to be set in the past, present or future?"

"Does your story have to have a happy ending?"

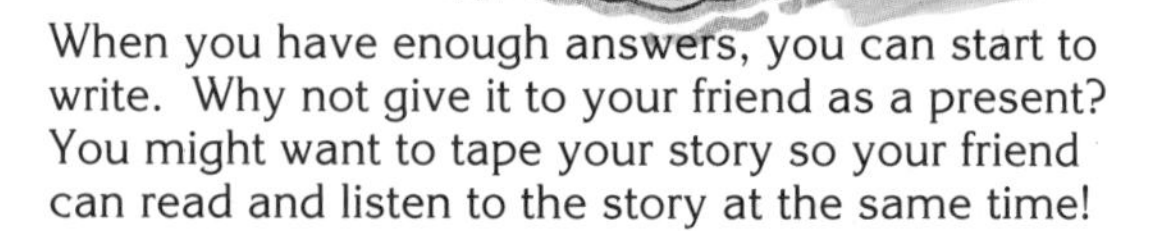

When you have enough answers, you can start to write. Why not give it to your friend as a present? You might want to tape your story so your friend can read and listen to the story at the same time!

ALL ABOUT ME

One of the most difficult but most interesting things to write about is yourself!

These days, many film stars and rock stars write their autobiographies (the story of their life) at a very young age, so why not have a go yourself?

You won't remember very much about your very early years but you can always ask your parents or other members of your family. Some of the things they tell you might not be very nice but it's never a good thing to take yourself too seriously.

You could try and write a little bit for each year of your life and you could illustrate your autobiography with photographs.

Try and find out what important events in history were happening at the time of your birth.

"I was born the day Liverpool won the league championship and the first space shuttle returned safely to earth."

As you get a little older, try and keep your autobiography up to date, so that when you ARE famous you won't have too much writing to do!

ALL SHAPES AND SIZES

Here are some ideas to make your poems and stories a little more shapely...

1, 2, 3, 4, 5.

See if you can write a story or poem that has one word on the first line, two words on the second and so on. When you get up to a high number like 12, you can start to count back to one!

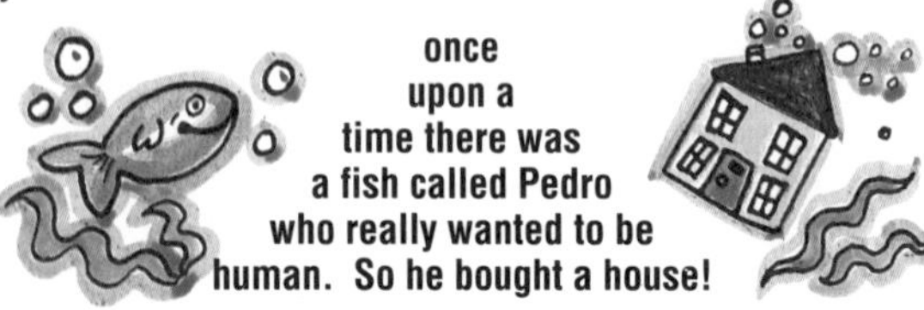

You could also start with 12 words and go down to one and then return to the number you started with. It's up to you!

Mountains

Here the words of your story or poem climb to the top and then descend the other side to make the shape of a mountain. Try and put the most important word in your writing at the top of the mountain.

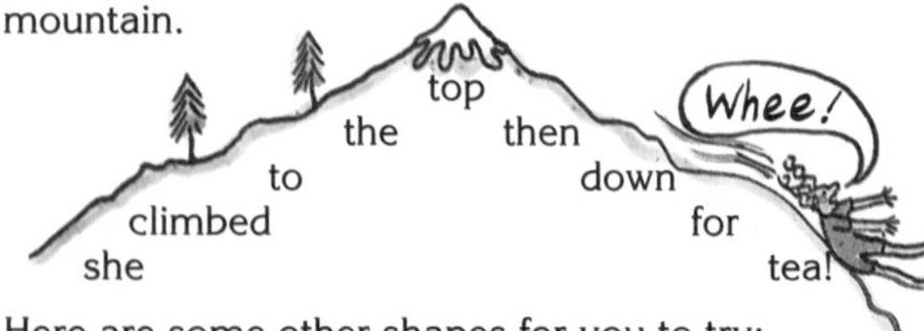

Here are some other shapes for you to try;
a waterfall / a winding staircase / a stormy sea.

Poetry pet

Copy out your story or poem about, say, a cat, in the shape of a cat. Draw round the outline of the pet you choose to write about and when you've finished copying out the words, you can rub out the outline so the words themselves make the shape of the animal!

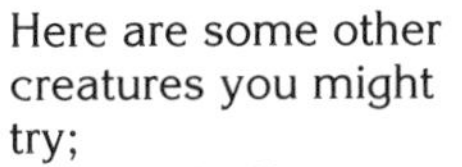

Here are some other creatures you might try;

a giraffe
a snake
a fish

Calligrams

This is when you write a word in the shape of its meaning. So you might choose to write the word 'spaghetti' in twisty letters that look like spaghetti being served on a plate!

Here are some words that make great calligrams;

balloon
catapult
crash

THE SENSES

As a writer, you need to be able to use all five of your senses so that you can describe things as fully as possible. Here are some ideas to help you sharpen up each sense!

Hearing

Choose a piece of "very" music; very loud, very soft, very romantic, very frightening, very strange...as long as it's very something! Classical music will give you lots of choices but don't forget jazz or pop. Songs with words might stop your imagination flowing.

Have a large sheet of plain paper so that you can write (or draw) whatever comes into your mind as you listen to the music.

- **pictures**
- **colours**
- **places**
- **people**
- **memories**

You might end up with a very crowded sheet of paper or just a few precious words. Whatever you have could be the starting point for a poem or a story. Or you might like to leave it as it is!

Some music you might like to try;

-Beethoven.Symphony No.9 (first movement)

-Rachmaninov. Piano Concerto No.2 (second movement)

-Jazz music by Miles Davis or Keith Jarrett.

Feeling
Different things have different textures. Make a collection of everyday objects but make sure that their textures (the way they feel) are all somehow different from each other. Here are some objects you might choose;

a pineapple / a piece of felt / an egg / sandpaper

Now write a line to describe the texture of each object you have chosen. It might help to close your eyes when you feel each object so you are thinking about the way it feels and nothing else!

See if your friends can match each object with the description of its texture or see if they can guess the object just from your description of the way it feels.

Seeing
Choose one colour and look at all the different ways it appears in the world around you;

Blue is the colour of the sky
Blue is the colour of the sea
Blue is the colour of this pen!

Smelling
Again, choose something with a 'very' smell; the sea, a bunch of roses, tar. Write a poem using this pattern;

"The smell of...reminds me of..."

Why not draw a picture for each idea you have?

Tasting
Can you think of 10 ways to describe the taste of Marmite? Or 7 ways to describe the taste of raw onions? You'll probably find it easier to describe a nasty taste than a nice taste!

salty
biting
tingly
tangy
stingy

IT'S MAGIC!

Recipes

Here are some ideas for some unusual recipes. You might know the recipe for making pancakes and omelets, but do you know the recipe for making happy children?

Mix a very long holiday with bright sunshine.
Pour the mixture into a park filled with 700 swings!
Add extra pocket money and stir with free sweets.

You'll soon get the idea. How about writing a recipe for a happy school or a recipe for brilliant parents? You can be as crazy as you like but don't forget you're writing a recipe!

Why not write a mini book of 'special' recipes and illustrate it with mad drawings of the results of your 'cookery'?

Potions

These are wonderful because you can put absolutely anything into your potion and choose exactly what you want it to do! You can have;
A potion to turn fish into opera stars
A potion to make footballers hate scoring goals
A potion to make the Prime Minister talk backwards.

Now for the ingredients;
Here are some suggestions.

page 47 of a boring book
nine spoonfuls of dirty bath water
a thin slice of a smelly slipper.

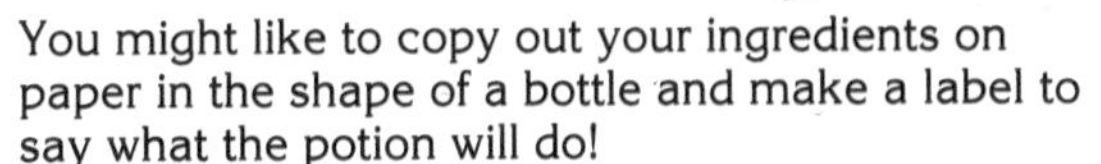

You might like to copy out your ingredients on paper in the shape of a bottle and make a label to say what the potion will do!

Instructions
You normally read instructions for boring things like tests at school but you could write rather magical instructions for almost anything!

Instructions for building a snowman

1.Wait for snow to fall.

2.Find your scarf and gloves.

3.Walk outside with a spade and a carrot.

You could write instructions for finding a ghost, for checking there's nothing under your bed at night, or for getting out of trouble for eating the last chocolate biscuit!

Riddles
This is where you become the thing you're describing and other people have to guess what you are!

I am black and white and read all over.
What am I? ***(a newspaper)***

Try and think up some riddles of your own - the stranger the better!

READ ALL ABOUT IT!

Have you ever wanted to be a journalist and run your own newspaper? Well, here are some ideas to get you started!

Shape and size
It's probably best to start with just one page so you don't have any empty spaces. Use a sheet of plain paper and work out where you're going to have the words and the pictures. Arrange the page like a jigsaw - and don't put anything down until you're happy with the layout of the whole page!

Headlines
These must stand out clearly,so use bubble letters or cut out letters from an old newspaper. It might take time but it's be worth it. Try and make your headlines memorable - there was one in a paper a few years ago about a flock of birds who kept making a 'mess' whenever they flew over an airport. It read, "The stains from cranes fall mainly on the planes!".

What kind of news?
1. National news
If you're really interested in the important stories of the day then why not write your own version of events? You could tape the news off the radio and then make up your mind which news you want to include in your own newspaper. You could use photographs from the daily papers but write your own captions for them!

2. Local news

Here you could interview people in your road about important local topics such as bus services, or how good the local shops are. You could have a 'What's on?' guide, telling your readers about jumble sales and school concerts. If you have a camera, you can include real pictures of a local football match or a wedding!

3. Fantasy news

You could write the news from an imaginary town (see page 11) and pretend your drawings are photographs. Your headlines could range from "Princess to marry frog" to "Teddy bear to become Prime Minister". You could have a pretend problem page with questions like, "I've been a wizard here for the past seven years but my spells won't work any more. Can you help?".

Page fillers

Here are some ways you can fill up any spare space you might have before your paper is ready; crosswords, wordsearches, cartoons, jokes ... even your own review of childrens' T.V!

Acrostics
You've probably written acrostics at school, without perhaps realising they were acrostics! This is where the title of the poem is written vertically in capital letters and each letter is used as the beginning of each horizontal line of the poem;

> An acrostic
> Can
> Really
> Offer you
> Some
> Tremendous poetic
> Ideas,
> Can't it?

The problem with acrostics is that teachers sometimes get you to do them when they can't think of any better ideas for poetry, so the poems can be quite boring. But if you think of some really unusual ideas, they can work wonderfully. Forget acrostics about 'Autumn' and 'Easter' - why not try out words like 'marshmallow' or 'dentist'? You could even use the acrostic as a way to remember a word with a mean spelling!

Alphabets
This is a good way of grouping similar ideas into one poem. You'll have seen animal alphabets before;

A is for Alligators always asking advice.

B is for Buffalo bursting blue balloons.

C is for Centipede counting corn-plasters.

You can have great fun drawing a funny picture for each letter. If you can't think of an animal for some letters, then make one up! There are also alphabet story poems, which can get in a really mad tangle the further along the alphabet you go;

Annie
Bought
Chocolate
Dinosaurs
Every
Friday!

Use a dictionary to collect ideas for each letter before you start. Copy your poems into little books with a letter on each page!

I am

Here's an unusual way to write a poem about yourself. Put a piece of plain white paper on a wall and shine a light onto it (an anglepoise light is best). Put your face between the light and the paper so that a small, sharp silhouette appears on the paper. Ask a friend to carefully draw round your shadow with a black pen. Try to keep as still as possible!

Copy your poem onto the paper so that you have a poem about you in the shape of you. Try to be as honest as possible in your writing. If you hate being kissed by your Auntie, then say so!

Love is...

... giving someone your last toffee. But it's also a million other things - some soppy, some serious, some silly, some sad. Try writing your own 'Love is' messages. Copy them onto paper cut into the shape of a heart!

RED LETTER DAY

A red letter day is a day which is special in some way. Here are some ideas to help you celebrate them!

Birthdays

You might have heard the phrase 'Each year a little older, a little wiser,' but is it true? Try and find time each birthday to do a little writing. You could keep a secret birthday book that you only use once a year. You might include;

'What I love doing.'
'What I hate doing.'
'My favourite places.'
'My least favourite places.'

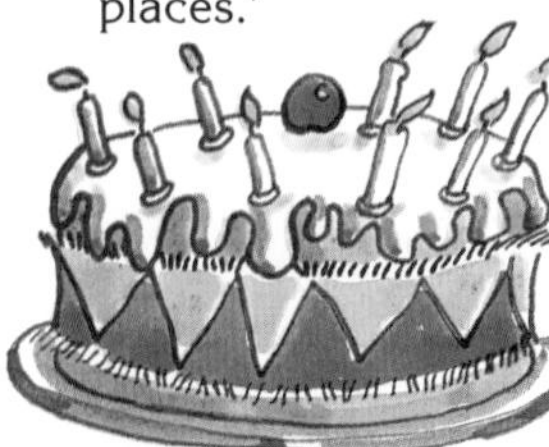

Try not to look at your birthday book except on your birthday. It will be a good way to see how quickly you change your ideas over the years!

Bank Holiday

A bank holiday sometimes means a day trip to the seaside, to the forest, to a museum or to the countryside. Wherever you go, try and bring back as many mementos of that day as possible. So, a day out at the seaside might end up with a bag filled with;

a train ticket
some seaweed
a candyfloss stick
a postcard.

When you get home, stick your 'momentos' carefully onto paper or card to make a 'picture poem'. You won't need to write any words because your momentos will say everything. All you need is a good title!

ODDS and ENDS

Book of Ideas

If you want to be a good photographer, you always carry a camera so you never miss a shot. If you want to be a good writer, always try to carry a little book so that if you suddenly have a brilliant idea you can write it down before you forget it!

Ideas can happen in the strangest places. On a bus, in a supermarket, even in a toilet. So be prepared!

Book of Quotes

The way you write depends on lots of things - especially on what you read. If there's a word or a sentence in a book that you really like (because it's funny, beautiful, strange or sad,) then write it down because it will help you to build up good ideas and to have an interesting vocabulary. You could also include interesting things you overhear on the radio, television and even between two people waiting for a train!

...ing sentences
Here's a rather strange idea that might help you to think about how important it is to put words in the best order possible (or the best possible order!). Find a very boring sentence in a very boring book and copy it out onto paper in quite big writing.

Here's an example;

Now cut out all the words and see if you can rearrange them to make crazy, weird sentences! Such as;

See how many crazy sentences you can discover in one boring sentence.

A long story in little bits
Charles Dickens published his novels in magazines and each episode would always end at a very exciting bit so the reader would want to buy the next magazine to see what happened next. Sometimes readers would wait excitedly in the streets for the new magazine to be on sale!

You could try writing a story in episodes yourself. Always make sure that the end of each episode will leave your reader hungry for more, such as,"He walked slowly down the corridor. Somebody was following...

END OF PART 65. FIND OUT WHAT HAPPENS NEXT WEEK!"

Send your story to a friend.
You could make it go on for years!!